Soldier's Heart

Soldier's Heart

David French

Talonbooks
2002

Talonbooks
P.O. Box 2076, Vancouver, British Columbia, Canada V6B 3S3
www.talonbooks.com

Typeset in New Baskerville and printed and bound in Canada.

Second Printing: August 2005

Rights to produce *Soldier's Heart*, in whole or in part, in any medium
by any group, amateur or professional, are retained by the author.
Interested persons are requested to apply to his agent: Charles
Northcote, The Core Group, 3 Church Street, Suite 507, Toronto,
Ontario M5E 1M2; Tel.:(416) 955-0819; Fax:(416) 955-0861.

On the cover: *PANL NA 2751—Newfoundland Regiment Section 2,
Platoon 1* is reprinted with the permission of The Provincial Archives
of Newfoundland and Labrador.

Keep The Home Fires Burning by Lena Gilbert Ford & Ivor Novello © 1914
(Renewed) Ascherberg, Hopwood and Crew. All rights for Canada
controlled by Chappell & Co. All Rights Reserved. Used by permission,
Warner Bros. Publications U.S. Inc., Miami FL 33014.

National Library of Canada Cataloguing in Publication Data

French, David, 1939-
 Soldier's heart

 A play.
 ISBN 0-88922-463-3

 I. Title.
PS8561.R44S64 2002   C812'.54   C2002-910064-X
PR9199.3.F73S64 2002

The publisher gratefully acknowledges the financial support of the
Canada Council for the Arts; the Government of Canada through the
Book Publishing Industry Development Program; and the Province
of British Columbia through the British Columbia Arts Council for
our publishing activities.

For Urjo Kareda
1944–2001

Soldier's Heart premiered at the Tarragon Theatre on November 13, 2001, with the following cast:

JACOB MERCER. . . . . Darren Keay
BERT TAYLOR . . . . Randy Hughson
ESAU MERCER. . . . . Oliver Becker

Directed by Bill Glassco
Set and Costumes designed by Sue LePage
Lighting designed by Robert Thomson
Sound designed by Evan Turner

CHARACTERS

Jacob Mercer, 16
Bert Taylor, 35
Esau Mercer, 40

PLACE

The platform of the railway station at Bay Roberts, Newfoundland.

TIME

Monday, June 30, 1924.

Soldier's Heart is to be played without intermission.

Hour after hour they ponder the warm field
And the far valley behind, where buttercups
Had blessed with gold their slow boots coming up.
    —Wilfred Owen, *Spring Offensive*

*The platform of the railway station at Bay Roberts,
Newfoundland.*

*Upstage is the exterior wall of the station. In the
clapboard wall is a door that opens into the station
proper. On either side of the door is a window of
translucent glass behind which the glow of electric
lights can be seen.*

*On the platform, close to the door, is a small wooden
bench. Stage left is a hand dolly for carting baggage.
Beside the dolly are a steamer trunk and a couple of
wooden boxes ready for transporting. A push-broom
leans against the wall.*

It is Monday, June 30, 1924; night.

*At rise, JACOB MERCER sits on the bench, a cloth cap
on his head, an old brown suitcase beside his feet ...
JACOB looks agitated. He sits with his elbows on his
knees, puffing on a tailor-made cigarette.*

*From the station-master's house abutting the station,
a First World War song plays softly on a gramophone:
"Keep The Home Fires Burning."*

*The station door opens and BERT TAYLOR enters.
BERT is dressed in his station-master's dark blue
uniform, brass buttons glinting ... For a moment or
two he stands in the doorway, studying JACOB, his
cap tilted back.*

BERT:

Looks like a slow night, Jacob. So far you're the only one who's bought a ticket.

JACOB:

Dammit, Bert, how come the train's always late?

BERT:

Not *always*, now. And listen, don't be running her down or she'll get a bad name. A bad name's as hard to remove as a birthmark.

JACOB:

(beat) Sadie sure likes those War songs, don't she?

BERT:

They remind her of England … Did I tell you? The Regiment sang that song the night we marched from Louvencourt to the Somme. Eight years ago tonight.

JACOB:

Bet you was scared, Bert.

BERT:

A man who says he wasn't is a liar … On our way to the Front we passed some soldiers coming back. One went: *'Baa! Baa!'* The next morning we learned what he meant.

JACOB:

Lambs to slaughter?

BERT:

Exactly.

> *The song ends. JACOB crushes out his cigarette. He walks to the edge of the platform … checks his pocket-watch.*

JACOB:

Maybe it galls you to hear it, Bert, but of all the crack passenger trains in North America, the Caribou's still the slowest.

BERT:

See that? It's smart alecks like you that give her a black eye.

JACOB:

(slyly) Sure, it's no secret how slow she is. She's even mentioned in the Bible.

BERT:

She is like hell.

JACOB:

The Book of Genesis.

BERT:

You're making that up.

JACOB:

Chapter 1, Verse 25: 'God made every t'ing that creepeth upon the earth.'

BERT:

Laugh all you want … Perhaps the Caribou don't always arrive on time, but dammit, she has a lot to contend with. And year round, too.

JACOB:

Like what?

BERT:

Like the snow at Gaff Topsails, for one. Or the winds at St. Andrews and Wreckhouse. Why, those winds come screeching down off Table Mountain so swift they can blow boxcars into the sea. Even a bull moose can derail the train. In rutting season

he'll charge the engine … Your father must've
mentioned it.

JACOB:

No.

BERT:

He didn't?

JACOB:

No, he didn't … I talk to you and Sergeant Kelly
more than him.

BERT:

Well, I don't see that much of him myself. As you
know, we seem to have lost touch.

JACOB:

Welcome to the club.

Pause.

BERT:

What happened today, Jacob? The two of you get in
a row? Is that it?

JACOB:

Why? What makes you say that?

BERT:

I'm not stupid. I sold you a ticket to St. John's,
didn't I? A one-way ticket … Besides, it's July 1st
tomorrow. We both know how that day can set him
off.

JACOB:

He can't seem to help himself.

BERT:

I know. I remember when he worked as a
Trainman. Our first year back from overseas ... We
had a runaway train that winter: the engineer had
died at the switch. No one knew it till the Caribou
began her run down from the Cat Hills and was
picking up too much speed ... Bet he never told
you that story, did he?

JACOB:

No.

BERT:

Esau was in the caboose. He scrambled up the
ladder and along the top, the walkway slippery with
ice, the train snapping like a shutter in the wind.
Got to the engine just in time. Just before we hit
the curve.

JACOB:

Christ, Bert.

BERT:

Wonder he wasn't killed ... Of all the jobs on the
train, the Trainman has the most dangerous. And
you know what, my son? I figure that's why he
wanted it.

JACOB:

Father?

BERT:

Just don't tell him I said that, you hear? He might
take it the wrong way.

JACOB:

Why? How might he take it?

BERT:

Well, he might think I meant he was trying to ...
You know.

JACOB:

What?

BERT:

No odds. Don't suppose he'd ever do something
like that, would he? Not on purpose.

JACOB:

Do what? Take his life?

BERT:

Keep your voice down! ... Now I never said that,
did I? It's just that ...

JACOB:

What? *(Then)* What, Bert?

BERT:

Nothing. Let's just drop it ... *(He begins to sweep the
platform with the push-broom)*

JACOB:

(pursuing him) Don't let on I mentioned it, okay?
Not even to Sadie, promise? But sometimes ...
sometimes he talks to Uncle Will.

BERT:

Oh?

JACOB:

It's mostly this time of year. Whenever he's had too
much to drink.

BERT:

What's he say to Will? You any idea?

JACOB:

I don't have a clue. Why?

BERT:

(*evasively*) No reason. Just wondered.

JACOB:

Mother makes me leave the moment it starts. She
hates me to see him that way ... This year, for the
first time, Uncle Will appeared to him in dreams.
She says he calls to Father from the Church of
England cemetery in Coley's P'int.

BERT:

Sure, Will's not buried here, he's buried in France.
Your father and I dug his grave. Hung his helmet
on his rifle butt, along with his identity disc.

JACOB:

... Mother said she woke up last night and Father
was gone. She found him up in the churchyard,
waving a Luger at the sky. The one he brought back
from the War.

BERT:

Christ Almighty.

JACOB:

It's loaded, too. He sleeps with it under his pillow.

BERT:

Yes, well, Will's death on July 1st, it ... I suppose it
ripped the heart right out of Esau. Worse, it made
him reckless.

JACOB:

Why? What would he do?

BERT:

Crazy things, mostly. Stuck his head up once, to get a sniper to shoot at him so we'd know where the bugger was hiding … The bullet combed his hair.

JACOB:

He won't speak about the War, you know. Not even to Mother. I've tried to coax him, but he won't.

BERT:

A lot of men won't, sure.

JACOB:

You will.

BERT:

Yes, I find it helps to talk about it.

JACOB:

It might help Father, too, mightn't it? *(Then)* Mightn't it, Bert?

BERT:

It might … Then again, it might not.

JACOB:

What's that supposed to mean?

BERT:

It's just that each man's experience was his own. Take me, now. I never lost a brother at the Somme. Nor was I badly wounded there like Esau … The Newfoundland Regiment was wiped out at Beaumont Hamel, but I got off without a scratch.

JACOB:

Still, I don't get it. You saved his life there, but now he barely speaks to you. Explain that.

BERT:

It's not for me to explain.

JACOB:

You must have some idea.

BERT:

Perhaps he didn't want to be saved, Jacob. Perhaps
it's as simple as that ... And listen, don't be making
me out a hero. The real heroes are the ones who
never came back. Like your Uncle Will. *(He
continues sweeping)*

> *Just then, ESAU MERCER appears in the doorway,
> though neither JACOB nor BERT notice ... ESAU is
> dressed in a worn tweed jacket and pants, a scuffed-
> up pair of black shoes on his feet. He wears a salt-
> and-pepper cap. A good-looking man, there is never-
> theless something unsettling about him. Maybe it's the
> pain in his eyes. An almost haunted look.*

JACOB:

Don't forget, Bert, I was at Sergeant Kelly's wedding ... When you showed up at the church, I was
standing next to Father. I saw the look he gave you.
And it wasn't hate or anger in his eyes, it was ...

BERT:

What?

JACOB:

I can't put my finger on it ... I just know that as
soon as he saw you, he turned and walked away.
Why'd he do that? And don't tell me it's 'cause you
saved his life. I don't buy it.

ESAU:

Go on, Bert. Tell him what he wants to know. It's
probably burning up your tongue.

Silence. ESAU and BERT exchange a look.

BERT:
How long have you been there, Esau?

ESAU:
Long enough ... That how you kills time? How you amuses the customers? Parading about the platform, boasting how you was Mentioned in Despatches?

BERT:
Indeed it's not.

ESAU:
'It was the first night of the Somme, folks. Private Mercer was wounded in No Man's Land. I slung him over my shoulder like a sack of flour and lugged him back to our lines.' ... That what you tells Sadie? She must be some impressed, married to a bona fide war hero.

BERT:
You're drunk, Esau.

ESAU:
I've been drinking; I ain't drunk. *(He sits on the bench, removes a hip flask from his jacket, and takes a drink)*

JACOB:
He wasn't bragging, Father. I'm the one who mentioned it first, not him.

ESAU:
No mistake.

JACOB:
It was, wasn't it, Bert?

BERT:

Stay out of it, now. There's no need to be taking sides on my account. It's not worth it. *(He leans the push-broom against the wall and exits)*

Pause. ESAU returns the flask to his jacket and gets to his feet.

ESAU:

All right, Jacob, now hand it over. Let's not make a scene in front of Bert.

JACOB:

Hand what over?

ESAU:

Don't be playing games. Give it here.

JACOB:

I don't have it.

ESAU:

Didn't you t'ink I'd notice it was gone? Or did you t'ink you'd be gone before I noticed? ... *(He pats JACOB down)* ... Where is it? Your suitcase?

JACOB:

No. I tossed it off the bridge, coming across the Klondyke. The bullets, too.

ESAU:

Show me. Open the suitcase.

JACOB:

No.

ESAU:

Open it, I said!

JACOB:

No.

ESAU sizes him up. Then he takes out his jackknife and attempts to pry open the locks.

JACOB:
Why'd you bring the Luger home, Father? You'm not the type to keep souvenirs. Like Sergeant Kelly with his German helmet.

ESAU:
I took that Luger from a man I killed at the Somme. It ain't a souvenir.

JACOB:
No? What is it, then? … And why do you always keep it loaded? Why?

Frustrated, ESAU puts away the jackknife. He takes the suitcase in his bare hands and rips it open.

JACOB:
It ain't there, Father. I already told you: I pitched it into the sea.

ESAU searches through the suitcase: no Luger … He unfolds a shirt. Inside is a framed photograph.

ESAU:
What's this doing in your suitcase?

JACOB:
Mother gave it to me. She said Uncle Will took it when you was both on leave in London. A few weeks before the Somme … That's his shadow on the ground.

ESAU studies the photo a moment, running his fingers over the surface. Then he places it back in the suitcase and closes the lid.

ESAU:

> What is it, Jacob? Revenge? That why you'm
> sneaking off like this? Like a t'ief in the night?

JACOB says nothing.

ESAU:

> Not man enough to tell me to my face? Is that it?
> Had to make your escape on the sly?

Again, JACOB says nothing.

ESAU:

> Answer me, dammit! I'm talking to you!

JACOB:

> I wasn't sneaking off.

ESAU:

> That you wasn't.

JACOB:

> I wasn't ... I told Mother I'd write.

ESAU:

> You didn't say a word to me, did you? Not a blessed
> word. Just packed your bag and headed for the
> station, without so much as a wave of the hand. All
> 'cause we had a falling out.

JACOB:

> A falling out? It was a lot more than that, Father. A
> lot more than a simple little row.

BERT returns with a dustpan. He sweeps up the dust.

ESAU:

> *(to BERT, finally)* Jacob spends more time here at
> the Bay Roberts station than he spends at home.
> What's he do? Talk your ear off? At home he's that
> sullen he barely says two words.

JACOB:

It's you who hardly speaks, not me!

ESAU:

Watch your tongue, you! I'm still your father! Speak to me in that tone of voice and I'll—

JACOB:

(cutting in) What?

BERT:

He's sixteen years old, Esau. He wants to know what we did overseas. It's only natural ... Remember that British recruiting poster? 'Daddy, what did you do in the Great War?'

ESAU:

What is it you tells him? How we sailed off in 1914 to save the world? You, me, and Will?

BERT:

Some saviours.

ESAU: *(recites bitterly)*

'Why did we j'in the Army, b'ys?
Why did we j'in the Army?
Why did we come to France to fight?
We must have been bloody well barmy.'

BERT:

The world was different then.

JACOB:

Don't forget, Father. Most believed the War would be over by Christmas.

ESAU:

Yes, Will wanted to go to Boston that fall with young Ruby Parsons. It was me who talked him out of it. 'It'll be a lark,' I said. 'We'll box the Kaiser's ears. Make ourselves a few dollars.'

BERT:
We had our heads up our arses, all of us.

ESAU: *(recites)*
>'Kaiser Bill went up the hill
>To play a game of cricket
>The ball went up his trouser leg
>And hit his middle wicket.'

(He takes a pull on the flask) Little did we know what lay ahead ...

JACOB:
(desperate to keep his father talking) Bert says the Regiment was made up of sailors and fishermen, office workers, lumbermen, teachers. Men from places like Heart's Delight and Tickle Harbour.

BERT:
Some couldn't read or write, sure.

JACOB:
You drilled on the old cricket pitch at Pleasantville. On October 4th, you sailed out of St. John's aboard the little *Florizel*, the smallest ship in the fleet.

BERT:
She'd been to the seal fishery that spring and stank like hell ... One day I went on deck to get a breath of air. There was a lad there from Witless Bay: Gus Pritchard. *(To ESAU)* Remember?

ESAU:
He wasn't from Witless Bay, Gus. He was from down near Burnt Cove.

BERT:

No odds. I saw him bent over the rail. At first I
thought he was sick. Then I leaned over and saw
what he was staring at.

JACOB:

What was it, Bert? Porpoises?

BERT:

No, not that day ... Perhaps your father can tell
you. He was on deck at the time.

JACOB:

What was Pritchard looking at, Father? *(Then)*
Father?

ESAU:

(beat) Horses.

JACOB:

Horses?

ESAU:

Dead Cavalry horses. Bobbing along our port side.

BERT:

The *Florizel* had met up with a convoy from Canada.
We travelled in three lines, a British battle ship
ahead of us, a cruiser behind. Three ships ahead in
our line—the port line—was the *Montezuma*. She
had a thousand horses aboard. Some perished on
the 11-day trip to England. Suffocated down below.

JACOB:

And they pitched them overboard?

ESAU:

Four or five a day in our line.

BERT:

The men got awfully quiet, didn't they, Esau? Some put down their playing cards. The sight of those horses floating past made them uneasy, suddenly ...

ESAU:

Some men gathered at the stern. There wasn't a sound on deck, except for the hiss of the ship slicing the water. The wake went out behind us for half a mile. And in the foam you could see these ... these beautiful Cavalry horses turning in slow circles. Twisting like dead leaves in the white of the wake ...

Silence. And in the silence a sprightly War song begins to play on the gramophone: "It's a Long Way to Tipperary."

BERT:

Goddamn gramophone! I don't know why I allowed Sadie to talk me into buying it. She has no idea what those songs can do to a man.

ESAU:

You two don't speak about the War?

BERT:

Not about the Somme, if that's what you mean. Some things are off limits, remember? Even to wives ... *(He starts for the door)* Well, I'd best go check on the Caribou. The damn old train might have derailed again, for all we know. *(He exits)*

Pause. JACOB removes his belt. He slips it around the broken suitcase and cinches it.

ESAU:

(for something to say) No wonder she's late. She has more than 500 miles of narrow-gauge track. Her

average speed is 20 miles an hour … One time I saw old Bill Russell jump down from the first car, fill his pail with blueberries, then leap back on before the caboose crawled in sight. Imagine.

The song ends (as if BERT has abruptly removed the record).

JACOB:
You didn't walk here in the dark of night to tell me that, did you? Or to get back that German Luger?

ESAU:
… Your mother was hoping I could talk some sense into you before the train arrives. She knows how hot-headed you can be.

JACOB:
Hot-headed?

ESAU:
And stubborn … Reconsider, why don't you? There's no need to be doing this, in spite of what happened this morning.

JACOB:
No?

ESAU:
What I did was wrong, Jacob. I'm the first to admit it … I don't know why it happened, I swear.

JACOB:
You could've killed me, Father.

ESAU:
Don't say that … I've been up in the woods all day, walking around. When I got back just now, your mother was sitting in the dark. I said, 'What is it, Rachel?' She said, 'He's gone.' … I didn't know

what she meant ... 'Gone? Who's gone?' 'Jacob,' she said. The way she whispered your name, I could tell she'd never forgive me.

JACOB:
That's all in your head, you know.

ESAU:
Don't be telling me what's in my head! You have no idea what's in my head! You *or* your mother!

JACOB:
How could we? You hardly say a word to us from one day to the next.

ESAU:
That's a lie.

JACOB:
Is it?

ESAU:
Well, I'm speaking to you now, ain't I? And goddammit, it's like pulling teeth! Worse!

Pause.

ESAU:
By the way, what'd you expect to do in St. John's? Curl up on a park bench? Sleep in some doorway like a lost dog?

JACOB:
I can look after myself.

ESAU:
Yes, you can so.

JACOB:
I can.

ESAU:

You'm only fifteen years old, Jacob. Fifteen!

JACOB:

I'm sixteen. I turned sixteen two weeks ago. Even Bert Taylor knows that.

ESAU:

Sixteen's still a boy.

JACOB:

I'll find a boarding-house. I'll get a job.

ESAU:

What job? Work is scarce. Veterans like me can't find work out there.

JACOB:

I'll manage.

ESAU:

For Christ's sake, I wouldn't harm a hair on your head. You knows that, don't you? ... What happened this morning was an accident, pure and simple.

JACOB:

(incredulous) An accident?

ESAU:

You'm old enough now to forgive and forget. You'm sixteen years old: a grown man.

JACOB:

You put a knife to my t'roat, Father! A knife! ... How could you do that? I'm your son!

ESAU:

I swear I don't know how it happened ... I was in
the barn, sharpening my jackknife, when you
walked up behind me. You must've startled me.

JACOB:

I was looking in your eyes. You didn't know who I was.

ESAU:

It all happened so fast. It was like I was still ...

JACOB:

What, Father? Still back in the War?

ESAU:

It must've been the rum I had this morning.
Sometimes too much can—

JACOB:

(cutting in) Don't make excuses, okay? It's not the
rum that's to blame, it's whatever happened to you
in France. Admit it.

ESAU:

Why? What's Bert been saying?

JACOB:

About what? *(Then)* About what, exactly?

ESAU:

He can't be trusted, you know. Sometimes he gets
t'ings wrong.

JACOB:

Like what? The time you saved the Caribou? Or the
time he saved your life? Which?

ESAU:

That's enough, now. I warned you before. Don't
speak to me like that, or else.

JACOB:

What'll you do? Strike me? The way you struck
Henry Sparkes and broke his jaw?

ESAU:

Henry Sparkes deserved what he got.

JACOB:

The Railway didn't agree. They fired you for
assaulting a Conductor ... Lucky for you Henry was
too scared to press charges.

ESAU:

He tossed firecrackers behind me. Wanted to see if
I'd hit the station floor ... A man like that's not
worth a pinch. He wouldn't have lasted one day of
basic training, let alone four years in the trenches.

JACOB:

Why? What was that like?

ESAU:

What? The trenches?

JACOB:

No. *(Beat)* Basic training.

ESAU:

(laughs) By God, Jacob, I got to hand it to you.
You'm a sly bugger, ain't you? You figures by getting
me to talk about Scotland, I'll talk about France ...
Besides, Bert's probably told you all about Scotland.

JACOB:

He told me some. He said you trained in the
Highlands. That's where you lost the first soldier:
John Chaplin. His appendix burst.

ESAU:

Yes, we buried him in a local churchyard, with full military honours. In those days we still behaved like human beings … *(He lights a cigarette, his hand trembling)*

JACOB watches him intently. Finally:

JACOB:

Bert says you took over Edinburgh Castle from the Royal Scots. He told me you drilled on the dunes beside the estuary. Or marched up around Arthur's Seat. Or over the Braid Hills to the south.

ESAU:

Bert didn't leave much out, did he? … What the hell you need me for? You seem to know it all.

JACOB:

I'd sooner hear it from you.

ESAU:

Must please him, to have someone besides Sadie hanging on his every word. Must make him feel like a father.

JACOB:

(not letting him change the subject) He said the best time in Scotland was the summer of 1915. That's when the Regiment moved to Stob's Camp, south of Edinburgh. You trained there before Gallipoli, didn't you? *(Then)* Didn't you, Father?

ESAU:

… We killed a lot of straw sacks with our bayonets. Marched 21 miles a day, with 50 pounds of gear.

JACOB:

Slept 12 to a tent.

ESAU:

> The weather was so nice, Will and me would sleep out under the stars ... It was at Stobs that I met my first German.

JACOB:

> Really?

ESAU:

> He wasn't much older than Will.

JACOB:

> Bert never mentioned it.

ESAU:

> There was an Enemy Detention Camp close by. Guarded by old men from the National Reserve ... None of us had seen a German. So one day Will and me walked the half-mile there and stood beside the fence. Wasn't long before this blond-haired lad sidles over. 'Hello there, kamerad,' he says. 'Can I bum a smoke?'

JACOB:

> What? In English?

ESAU:

> Don't look so surprised. He spoke it better than we did. *(A slight German accent)* 'I lived two years in Winnipeg,' he said. 'Six months in Montreal.'

JACOB:

> He mistook you for Canadians?

ESAU:

> Will set him straight. 'I'm no bloody Canadian, kamerad,' says Will. 'I'm one-hundred-percent British. As British as those guards there.' He didn't

want to be mistaken, Will didn't. Not even by the enemy.

BERT returns. On a tray he carries a tea service and a small photo album.

BERT:
Some good news, boys. I talked Sadie into putting the gramophone away for the night. *(He sets the tray on one of the boxes)* The bad news is Jack Rossiter just called. He's the stationmaster at Harbour Grace ... There's been an accident near there.

ESAU:
Oh?

BERT:
That's why the train's late.

JACOB:
What happened, Bert?

BERT:
She struck some fellow at a crossing. They've been searching for him under the cars.

ESAU:
Anyone we knows?

BERT:
No idea. They still haven't found the body.

JACOB:
How long will they be? Did he say?

BERT:
(pouring tea) Well, it's dark out. And they still have to comb both sides of the tracks ... Meanwhile, Sadie made us all a pot of tea ... *(Offers a cup to ESAU)* Esau?

ESAU:

I'll pass. *(He indicates the flask)*

JACOB:

Me, too, Bert.

BERT:

Can't say I blame you. Sadie makes the weakest tea
and the hardest old biscuits. She's like those Army
cooks. Their biscuits were more lethal than bullets.

ESAU:

Hark to him! Lethal! ... What's Sadie been up to
lately? Still learning you how to speak?

BERT:

(drinking tea) Teaching me, not learning me.

ESAU:

What?

BERT:

That's the proper way to say it. She calls it
grammar.

ESAU:

That a fact?

BERT:

I don't see the harm in it. Sadie believes in self-
improvement. *(To JACOB)* The day I met her, she
was serving sandwiches at the YMCA All-Welcome
Hut in London. I could tell she was a cut above the
rest.

ESAU:

In other words, she ignored him completely.

BERT:

Like hell she did.

ESAU:

Too bad you never met her sooner. You might've made General. Though why any man would want to be an officer is beyond me. The damn fool's a sitting duck.

JACOB:

Why is that, Father?

ESAU:

Why? 'Cause a sniper will always go for the officer before the Private, given a choice. And the higher the rank, the better. We learned that at Gallipoli ...
(Sings to the tune of "Pretty Redwing")
    'Oh, the moon shines bright on Charlie Chaplin
    His boots are crackin' for the want of blackin',
    And his baggy trousers they want mendin'
    Before they send him to the Dardanelles.'

(He takes a drink from the flask) Christ, what a baptism that was ...

JACOB:

(beat) Tell me about Gallipoli, Father ... I know it's a peninsula in Turkey. Bert showed it to me on a map.

ESAU:

Bert has too much time on his hands.

JACOB:

The campaign there was Winston Churchill's idea. He lost his job over it, didn't he?

BERT:

First Lord of the Admiralty.

ESAU:

> *(to BERT)* He don't need to hear about Gallipoli.
> He's just a youngster.

BERT:

> A youngster? He's sixteen years old.

ESAU:

> I knows how old he is. I'm his father.

JACOB:

> Sure, boys my age enlisted. Some died on the field
> of battle.

ESAU:

> A damn lot of good that did.

JACOB:

> It can't hurt to talk about the War, can it? It might
> even help to—*(He catches himself)*

ESAU:

> Help what? *(Then)* Help what?

> *JACOB says nothing.*

ESAU:

> Don't push your luck, my son. First it was Scotland
> you wanted to talk about; now it's Turkey. Next it'll
> be France, I suppose.

JACOB:

> I won't mention the Somme. I give you my word.

ESAU:

> I don't believe you. It ain't like you to give up. It
> ain't in your nature.

BERT:

> *(to JACOB)* By the way, I remembered those snaps I
> mentioned the other day. Sadie found them in the

trunk … *(He gets the album)* I might have a postcard
here of the *Megantic.*

JACOB:

The *Megantic?*

BERT:

The ship that took us to Turkey. Well, almost there.
The last of the trip was aboard the *Prince Abbas*, a
coastal steamer. *(To ESAU)* Remember?

ESAU:

… I minds we anchored 50 miles off Gallipoli, at
Mudros. Each man was handed a scrap of paper
and told to write his next of kin.

JACOB:

Next of kin?

ESAU:

No one liked the sound of those words.

BERT:

I almost soiled me pants.

ESAU:

The past year had seemed like a holiday. Drilling at
Pleasantville in our blue puttees, our khaki trousers
itching in the sun … the send-off in St. John's, the
bunting strung across Water Street, the crowds
cheering …

BERT:

… the trip across to England. The *Florizel* Glee
Club sang: *(He sings)*
  'My bonnie lies over the ocean,
  My bonnie lies over the sea.' …

ESAU:

> ... then marching across the Scottish hills, the bugle band scaring the sheep. It hadn't seemed real somehow. More like a game ... When they mentioned our next of kin, it was like a pan of ice water in the face.

BERT:

> The *Prince Abbas* headed for Gallipoli at 3:30 the next afternoon. A 5-hour trip. Almost from the start we heard what sounded like distant thunder.

JACOB:

> It wasn't, though, was it, Father?

BERT:

> No. The noise we heard was the rumble of Turkish guns. They were shelling the beaches at Suvla Bay. The beaches we were headed for ...

ESAU:

> Will and me stood on deck that day, Gallipoli getting closer with each dip of the bow ... Then night fell. I noticed my hand shook. I tried to spit but couldn't. I wondered if Will had the heart to kill someone. Someone like the lad near Stobs who'd come to the fence to bum a smoke ... It's easy to aim your rifle at a man. It ain't so easy to pull the trigger, watching him stumble and fall. Knowing he'll never rise again. Never get to his feet and brush himself off ... *(He takes another drink)*

BERT:

> None of us had ever fired a shot in anger.

ESAU:

> I minds climbing into the landing craft. It was called a lighter. It could hold 500 men and 50 horses. As we headed in to Kangaroo Beach, the

men got quiet. Quiet and still. Only the horses stirred, their shoes clicking on the steel floor of the lighter. Any second we expected to hear bullets clanging off the sides. It didn't happen. All we heard was the sound of the motor, and the *click-click* of the horses' hooves ...

BERT:
And then we hit the beach, and all hell broke loose. Johnny Turk began lobbing shells at us, the wounded dropping like flies.

ESAU:
...Welcome to Gallipoli, boys! Each man had half a pint of drinking water a day, it tasting of petrol. *(To BERT)* Tell him about the lice. Maybe he won't find war so damn romantic.

JACOB:
I don't find it romantic.

BERT:
We called it 'picking shirts.' We'd take our shirts off and pick the lice out of the seams. Or burn them out with candles.

ESAU:
One day Will ran naked into the sea, just to stop the itching. Even the fear of snipers couldn't slow him down ... Tell him about the flies.

BERT:
Don't remind me.

JACOB:
(to ESAU) What about the flies?

ESAU:
(to BERT) You tell him.

JACOB:

I'd sooner you did, Father.

ESAU:

Why's it important that I tell you?

JACOB:

It just is. *(To BERT)* No offence, Bert.

BERT:

None taken.

ESAU:

… Come October, the weather turned warm.
That's when the flies swept down on us. Like sheets
of black rain. They bred in the bodies in No Man's
Land … They'd get in your eyes and ears, your
nose, your food. It was like crunching bits of sugar.

JACOB:

Jesus.

ESAU:

War can wear you down. The monotony. The bore-
dom. Not knowing what's going on. Not'ing to read
but the odd letter from home. Week after week not
able to take off a stitch, not even your boots.

BERT:

It made grown men weep.

ESAU:

But the worst was yet to come: the November
Storm. The worst in 40 years, and us in our pith
helmets and shorts.

BERT:

The Army had decided to retreat, you see. They'd
sent our winter uniforms back to Mudros.

ESAU:

>November was supposed to be grand. Instead it was gale after gale. Then the big one hit, rain and all. Trenches flowed like rivers. The temperature dropped and the trenches froze. It was like that for two days. 200 British soldiers drowned or froze to death.

BERT:

>The Newfoundlanders were lucky. Only 150 went to hospital, your uncle included. Most from frost-bite.

ESAU:

>I prayed he'd lose a finger or toe. That way he'd be out of the War for good … It didn't happen. He was back in the trenches before we left for France … Young Ruby had sent him a snap of herself. His black-haired Ruby from Bareneed.

BERT:

>Don't keep dwelling on it, boy. What happened at Beaumont Hamel was not your fault.

ESAU:

>He was my brother, Bert. I was supposed to look after him. Instead, I—

BERT:

>*(cutting in)* Look, I don't think we ought to be discussing it right now … *(To JACOB)* Maybe your father's had a bit too much to drink.

ESAU:

>Don't be foolish.

JACOB:

>Father can drink the both of us under the table, Bert, and not slur a word.

ESAU:

Goddamn right! *(He drains the flask)* There. And I
can walk a straight line, too, better than you or
your buddy, Father Shipley. *(He demonstrates)* By the
way, I saw him last night, stumbling home,
slobbering on his chin. He almost walked off the
cliff.

BERT:

Go easy on the man, Esau. He went overseas, too,
remember ... Wait here, boy. Sadie keeps a bottle
for medicinal purposes. I could use a drop or two
myself. *(He picks up the tray and exits)*

    ESAU lights a cigarette. JACOB watches him.

JACOB:

Father?

ESAU:

What?

JACOB:

Talking about the War might do some good. It's a
way to let off steam.

ESAU:

A man ain't a machine, Jacob. Sometimes he breaks
in ways that can't be fixed ... Now give your tongue
a rest. You could talk a hole t'rough an iron pot
and still have words enough for the Lord's Prayer.

    Pause.

JACOB:

I spoke to Albert Dawson the other day. I dropped
by his forge ... As a Roman Catholic, Albert
believes in Confession.

ESAU:

Confession?

JACOB:

He says it's good for the soul.

ESAU:

I'm Church of England, not Roman Catholic. And
stay away from Albert Dawson, you hear? Next he'll
be trying to convert you.

JACOB:

Well, what about our new minister? The Reverend
Mr. Phillpot? I bet he's a good listener. Why,
yesterday he even cracked a joke.

ESAU:

Did he, now?

JACOB:

He said he once met a man from Joe Batt's Arm,
who'd made himself a fiddle. The man said to the
Reverend Phillpot, 'Reverend,' he said, 'I just made
this fiddle out of me own head, and I've enough
wood left to make another.'

ESAU frowns.

JACOB:

What? You don't get it?

ESAU:

No. Tell it again.

JACOB:

A second time won't help. Half the congregation
didn't get it, either.

ESAU:

> Besides, I don't attend church. You knows that. Not since I came back from overseas.

JACOB:

> Still, I bet the Reverend Phillpot would hear you out. The way Father Shipley listens to Albert … It's worth a try, ain't it?

ESAU:

> It's a waste of time … T'ings happen in war that can never be forgotten … never be forgiven. T'ings that a man just has to live with. It's his punishment. *(He drops his cigarette butt and crushes it underfoot)*

JACOB:

> Bert talks about the War. He says it helps him … Mostly, he confides in Sadie and me.

ESAU:

> Bert has a tongue on him like a miller's clapdish: it never stops … Sadie don't need to be reminded, and her with a cousin killed at Mons.

JACOB:

> He hardly ever cries out in his sleep, Father. And he's never once climbed out of bed and walked in the Church of England cemetery.

ESAU:

> Who told you that? Your mother?

JACOB:

> She worries about you.

ESAU:

> No need to, sure.

JACOB:

> Why'd you take the Luger last night? It could've
> discharged and killed somebody.

ESAU:

> Who? Father Shipley serenading the stars? ... Your
> mother frets too much. Right now she's upset
> about you leaving.

JACOB:

> That ain't true.

ESAU:

> It ain't the half of it. She told me if I didn't bring
> you back not to bother coming home myself.

JACOB:

> She never said a word of that. And I can prove it.

ESAU:

> How?

JACOB:

> How? 'Cause she's the one who told me to pack my
> bag. After what happened this morning, she was
> afraid you'd do me harm. The way you hurt *her* that
> time.

ESAU:

> I didn't do that on purpose, and she knows it. I was
> lashing out in my sleep.

JACOB:

> You still broke her arm, didn't you? Even if you
> didn't mean to ... And look what you did to your-
> self that time. The day you was cutting pickets for
> the fence.

ESAU:

> You wasn't there. You was in school.

JACOB:
    Sergeant Kelly told me. He said he was with you in
the yard, when Mother let the back door slam. He
said the axe slipped out of your hand and sliced off
your nose. It was hanging down on your chin by a
piece of skin.

ESAU:
    The doctor sewed it back with a hair from the
horse's tail. He said, 'It's a good t'ing you have a
wife already, Esau, 'cause you'd never get one now.'
(He laughs)

        *BERT returns. He carries a bottle of whisky and two
        glasses.*

BERT:
    Don't tell Sadie we drank her Scotch. I'd never
hear the last of it ... *(He hands ESAU a glass and
pours him a drink)* While I was inside, I called
Harbour Grace. Jack says the man they thought was
killed there tonight wasn't killed at all.

ESAU:
    Oh?

BERT:
    His name is Angus Small. The name ring a bell?

ESAU:
    Not Corporal Small? Of 'C' Company?

BERT:
    That's him. Jack says he went over with the Second
Contingent. Lost a leg in France. A Mills bomb, he
thinks. *(He pours himself a drink)*

ESAU:
    No.

BERT:
No what?

ESAU:
It wasn't a Mills bomb, and it wasn't in France. He took a bullet the day our Regiment evacuated Gallipoli. The day we headed for France ... 'Lucky bugger,' Will said. 'That's a Blighty wound for sure.'

JACOB:
What's a Blighty wound?

ESAU:
One that got you sent to England ... No one expected he'd lose a leg. I saw him last year in St. John's. He was hobbling down Military Road, the leg of his pants pinned up behind ...

BERT:
(beat) According to Jack, the accident tonight was no accident.

ESAU:
What? ...

BERT:
The Engineer saw Angus step in front of the train just before she struck him ... Jack knows Angus. He suffers from soldier's heart. *(To JACOB)* What we now call shell-shock.

ESAU:
Still, that don't mean he tried to take his life. The man was on crutches. Maybe he tried to cross the tracks and froze.

BERT:

>They thought the same till they found his cap
>alongside the tracks.

ESAU:

>His cap?

BERT:

>Inside it were a pair of bifocals, an apple wood
>pipe, and a new set of false teeth. All neatly laid
>out.

ESAU:

>Jesus wept.

BERT:

>Then someone heard a noise; a moaning. And out
>crawled Angus from behind some bushes. Bloody
>but unbowed.

JACOB:

>Imagine.

BERT:

>Soon as he found he was all in one piece, he acted
>like a different man. Tipped his head back and
>laughed like hell. Jack says it's the first time anyone
>in Harbour Grace has heard Angus Small laugh in
>years ... Perhaps he realized it was good to be alive
>after all. In spite of his lost leg.

JACOB:

>Wouldn't it be great, Bert, if the War couldn't hurt
>him anymore? If he could put it all behind him?
>*(Then)* Wouldn't it, Father?

ESAU:

>Miracles like that don't happen.

BERT:

Dammit, Esau, let's drink to it anyway. *(Toasting)*
Here's to Corporal Small. To Corporal Small and
all the broken men just like him. May they find
some peace in their hearts at last. God knows they
deserve it.

ESAU:

Amen. To Corporal Small. The best Lewis gunner
in 'C' Company. *(They raise their glasses and drink)*

JACOB:

(beat) Father.

ESAU:

What?

JACOB:

I wouldn't mind a drop of liquor. I'm old enough
now. Ain't I, Bert?

BERT:

Whisky won't harm him none. Might put some hair
on his chest.

ESAU:

He don't need chest hair, he's barely sixteen ...
When did you say your birthday was?

JACOB:

June 12th.

ESAU:

Do you smoke yet?

JACOB:

Smoke? No.

ESAU:

Liar. I saw you the other day. You was puffing away
down by the coal-shed. *(To BERT)* I used to smoke at
his age. Hid my makings in the cliff. *(To JACOB)*
One time the Old Man caught me red-handed and
gave me the belt.

JACOB:

He did?

ESAU:

He'd preach about the evils of tobacco. How it
would stunt my growth and lead to the demon
rum. *(He hands JACOB his glass, a little Scotch still in
it)*

BERT:

Did it?

ESAU:

Let's put it this way. It didn't stunt my growth none.
(Laughs) Say, Bert, did you hear about the Pope and
Father Shipley? They'm out for a walk one day,
when the Devil drops down from a tree. The Pope
sits down and rolls up his pants. Father Shipley says,
'What're you doing?' The Pope says, 'What's it look
like? I'm getting ready to run.' Father Shipley says,
'Holy Father, no one can outrun the Devil.' The
Pope says, 'I don't have to, Shipley. I just have to
outrun *you*.'

BERT:

(laughs) Hell, the last time I heard that it was two
old hunters and a grizzly bear.

JACOB:

(suddenly) Listen …

BERT:

What?

JACOB:

Did you hear it?

ESAU:

Hear what?

JACOB:

For a second there, I ...

BERT:

Can't be the Caribou, if that's what you imagined.
The soonest you can hear the whistle is when she's
coming into Spaniard's Bay.

ESAU:

She could be quite a spell, couldn't she, Bert?
Might not make it till the small hours of the
morning.

JACOB:

I'll wait.

ESAU:

Dammit, Jacob, it ain't right. People will say I'm the
one who drove you away. It's me who'll have to live
it down.

JACOB:

Since when have you cared what other people said?

ESAU:

Even if you do make St. John's tonight, how will
you find a room? The city'll be fast asleep.

BERT:

Oh, I doubt that, Esau, considering what's
happening there tomorrow.

ESAU:

Why? What's happening?

BERT:

Didn't you hear? They're dedicating the National War Memorial. Even Sadie wants to go in.

ESAU:

It's the first I've heard tell of it ... I don't read the papers.

JACOB:

The parade's supposed to be the biggest ever. At least six marching bands ... They say Field-Marshall Haig will unveil the monument.

ESAU:

Haig?

BERT:

The Great Soldier himself. He arrived from England yesterday aboard the *Caronia*, him and the Countess.

ESAU:

Don't tell me Sir Douglas is now an earl?

BERT:

That's nothing. The British government gave him a gift after the War: a hundred thousand pounds.

ESAU:

Yes, well, I knows what I'd like to give him: the toe of my shoe up his arse. How can a man like that sleep at night? How can he lay his head on the pillow, with the slaughter of the Somme on his conscience? *(To JACOB)* 60,000 British soldiers fell on July 1st, and him 15 miles behind the front,

strutting about with his shiny boots and swagger
stick, not a hair out of place.

BERT:

For God's sake, Esau, the Commander-in-Chief
can't be expected to go over the top like a common
soldier.

ESAU:

Maybe that's the trouble. Maybe if he had to, he
wouldn't be so quick to send others...Here. Give
me that. *(He snatches the bottle from BERT and pours
himself a shot)* 20,000 dead, 40,000 wounded. For
that alone, Douglas Haig can kiss my ass, earl or no
earl! *(He knocks back the drink)*

Pause.

JACOB:

Father.

ESAU:

What now?

JACOB:

Look, I know I said I'd never mention France
again, but ...

ESAU:

But what?

JACOB:

It's *history*, Father. Eight years ago tonight, the
Newfoundland Regiment marched from the village
of Louvencourt to the Front. The weather was
good, remember? It rained the past five days, but
on June 30th, the sun came out.

BERT:

Jacob ...

JACOB:

You'd been billeted there since April. Since arriving from Gallipoli. You practiced in the wheat fields for the Big Push. It was supposed to be June 29th, but because of the rain, it was changed to July 1st ... You, Uncle Will, and Bert always stayed with the same family.

BERT:

Yes, when we went on leave.

JACOB:

They cried when you went to the Front that night. The children ran after you down the road, waving.

ESAU:

(to BERT) Who told him all that? You?

BERT:

I might have mentioned it in passing.

ESAU:

He remembers every word he hears, Bert. Every goddamn syllable.

BERT:

But don't you see, boy? It's not the War that he wants to understand, it's you.

ESAU:

Me?

BERT:

He wants his father back ... He's tried to talk to you in the past, but you walk away. That's why he sought out Sergeant Kelly and me ...

JACOB:

Besides, Bert scarcely mentioned the Somme. A word or two, maybe.

ESAU:

Like what?

JACOB:

Like the church at Albert. The Regiment passed it
on the road that night. What was it called? Nôtre
Dame de ... somet'ing.

ESAU:

How the hell should I know its name? A Catholic
church, no less.

JACOB:

Bert says it was you who p'inted it out.

ESAU:

Well, Bert's mistaken. His memory's not that sharp
at the best of times.

BERT:

(to JACOB) Listen, I don't think your father wants to
relive all that. Tonight of all nights.

JACOB:

No odds. It just came back to me: Nôtre Dame de
Brébières. *(To BERT)* Did I say it right?

BERT:

A lot better than I could.

JACOB:

Albert was only a mile or so from the Front ... A
gold statue of the Virgin Mary stood atop the
church tower. She was holding the baby Jesus up to
the sky. Uncle Will said it looked like she was
offering her son as a sacrifice. The way a lot of
mothers had done lately.

ESAU:

I don't recall Will saying that.

JACOB:
> A German shell had struck the tower the year
> before, the statue leaning at a right angle.

ESAU:
> So?

JACOB:
> So the soldiers called her the Gold Virgin. The
> Allies believed if she fell to the ground, the
> Germans would win the War. That's why the French
> put a chain on her to keep her up and the
> Germans tried to shoot her down.

ESAU:
> Which only proves how crazy both sides could be ...
> Now enough, Jacob. I didn't come here tonight to
> discuss some bombed-out church on the road to
> Beaumont Hamel.

JACOB:
> Bert said the Regiment sang "Keep The Home Fires
> Burning" the night you marched away from
> Louvencourt, into history.

ESAU:
> *(exasperated)* What am I going to do with him, Bert?
> He don't seem to hear!

JACOB:
> I hear. I just don't listen.

BERT:
> I think you're being unfair, Jacob. It's obvious your
> father can't talk about it ... One day he might be
> able to. Just not tonight.

JACOB:

> (*fiercely*) Don't you get it, Bert? It can't be some
> other night! It has to be this night!

BERT:

> Jacob ...

JACOB:

> No, goddammit! It's tonight or never!

ESAU:

> Watch your tongue, now ...

JACOB:

> Let me tell you somet'ing, Father. I remembers
> when Bert first mentioned the family you stayed
> with at Louvencourt. Do you know what it was I felt
> that day? Guess. (*Then*) Go on. Guess.

ESAU:

> What?

JACOB:

> Jealousy.

ESAU:

> Jealousy?

JACOB:

> I resented those two little French kids. You know
> why? 'Cause they'd spent time with you that I
> hadn't. Time before you pulled the world down
> over your ears and shut us all out.

ESAU:

> They didn't speak a word of English, those
> children.

JACOB:

What odds? They ran after you down the road, didn't they? ... The War took you from us, Father, in more ways than one. On the day you returned home, you made me a promise. A promise I've waited six years for you to keep. Well, I'm finished waiting. The train'll be here soon, and then it'll be too late.

ESAU:

(to BERT) What's the hell's he on about now? *(To JACOB)* What promise?

JACOB:

Remember that day? The day you stepped off the train here in Bay Roberts and walked across the Klondyke into Coley's P'int, your haversack over your shoulder? Remember?

ESAU:

It was a Sunday morning. I minds it.

JACOB:

Mother wasn't expecting you. She'd gone to church ... I had the colic, so I stayed home.

ESAU:

Some colic. He sat up there on Jenny's Hill, sunning himself. Like he owned the sky.

JACOB:

That's when I saw you below on the road. Not that I knowed you. It was the uniform I recognized, with the red triangle on the sleeve ... I watched you set down your canvas bag. You stood looking across the water at Bareneed.

ESAU:

> *(to BERT)* I was recalling our last night in Scotland.
> Will and me lay outside the tent and talked. It was
> the last time the stars ever looked friendly.

BERT:

> What did you talk about?

ESAU:

> Home, mostly. Will missed Ruby from Bareneed.
> *(To JACOB)* I missed you and your mother ... And
> yet home seemed different that Sunday morning. I
> noticed it the moment I stepped off the train.

JACOB:

> Different? How?

ESAU:

> Distant, I suppose. Familiar, yet strange ... I was
> trying to make sense of it all when I saw you climb-
> ing down from Jenny's Hill. *(To BERT)* I didn't know
> him, either. He was only six when I went overseas.

JACOB:

> I ran up to him, Bert. I asked if he knowed Esau
> Mercer of 'A' Company.

ESAU:

> 'He's one of the First Five Hundred,' he told me.
> 'One of the famous Blue Puttees.' 'Hell, I'm Esau
> Mercer,' I said. 'Who wants to know?'

JACOB:

> I said, 'Don't you recognize me, sir? I'm Jacob.
> Jacob Mercer, your son.' ... That's when you burst
> into tears, Father, standing there in that Sunday
> morning road with the bells ringing and the sea
> like a looking-glass. It's the only time I've ever seen
> you cry. It frightened me.

ESAU:

    (impatiently) What about the promise, Jacob?

JACOB:

    I haven't forgotten … I remembers when we got home, you scared me even more. You walked into the parlour and stared at the cabinet where Mother kept all her good china. Suddenly you swept your hand across the shelves and broke every cup and saucer, every plate that was in there. Even her little figurines.

ESAU:

    … It was all made in Germany.

JACOB:

    'My head's pounding,' you said. 'I'm going to lie down now … Tomorrow we'll talk, Jacob. That's a promise.'

ESAU:

    I said that?

JACOB:

    Those exact words. 'Tomorrow we'll talk, Jacob. That's a promise.'

ESAU:

    I don't recall.

JACOB:

    Funny, we've talked more tonight than in all the past six years. We've even talked about the War. But we still haven't mentioned the most important part of all: July 1st. And why it is you avoids Bert.

ESAU:

    (to BERT) Is that what you told him? That I've been dodging you?

BERT:

Indeed I didn't! I never said a word, did I, Jacob?

JACOB:

I'm no fool, Father. And I ain't blind ... Bert would never tell, but I'm sure he knows more than he's letting on. That's why you shuns him, ain't it? Like that time at Sergeant Kelly's wedding. It's almost as if ...

ESAU:

What?

JACOB:

As if you can't bring yourself to look at him ... *(A new thought)* Or is it that you can't bear to have *him* look at *you?* Which?

ESAU:

You tell me.

JACOB:

It's all connected to Uncle Will, ain't it? Somet'ing happened out there in No Man's Land that neither you nor Bert will talk about.

BERT:

Will died in battle, Jacob. He died and was buried. That's all that happened in No Man's Land.

JACOB:

I don't believe you ... For years, Father, you've kept it inside you, locked away like a dark secret. Whatever it is, it can't be so bad you can't speak about it.

ESAU:

Can't it?

JACOB:

> No.

ESAU:

> You've lived a sheltered life, my son.

JACOB:

> Maybe I have. But I'm sixteen now. A grown man, you called me. Old enough to forgive and forget.

ESAU:

> ... When we first came home, people didn't want to hear about the War. It had gone on too long. Sergeant Kelly once said to me, 'Esau, if you wants to empty a room, tell them what it was like over there. Tell it the way you couldn't in your letters.'

JACOB:

> Like what?

BERT:

> Like the night I bent down to pick a mushroom. Only it wasn't a mushroom I saw in the moonlight. It was a piece of white bone the rats had gnawed on.

> *Just then, the far-off cry of a train whistle pierces the night, the sound sharp and mournful.*

JACOB:

> That's the Caribou now. She'll soon be pulling into Spaniard's Bay. Next stop is Bay Roberts.

ESAU:

> Have you any idea what'll happen if you boards that train? You'll be breaking your mother's heart. The way I broke her Dresden china.

JACOB:
 Mother's stronger than you *or* me. Besides, she told
 me to go, remember. She helped me pack.

ESAU:
 Don't be stupid. She wanted to protect you. That's
 a different kettle of fish ... The house'll be like a
 morgue now. Like someone's died there.

JACOB:
 It's been like a morgue for years. You just haven't
 noticed.

ESAU:
 I've already lost a brother, Jacob. I don't want to
 lose a son ... If you gets on that train tonight, you
 may never return. Life is like that.

JACOB:
 Why do you care if I go? You scarcely give me a
 second glance. It's like I don't exist.

ESAU:
 It ain't that, Jacob, it's ... *(He turns away)*

JACOB:
 What?

ESAU:
 No odds. Let's say I didn't come here tonight just
 for your mother. Let's leave it at that.

 JACOB hesitates, then produces the train ticket.

JACOB:
 All right, Father, I'll make you a deal ... You
 listening?

ESAU:
 What?

JACOB:

Tell me what happened on July 1st, and I'll cash in this ticket. I'll sleep in my own bed tonight and never mention the War again. Not even to Bert. So help me God.

ESAU:

Don't go dragging God into it. He won't do you a bit of good.

BERT:

(to JACOB) He doesn't want to discuss July 1st. I think he's made that clear enough.

JACOB:

(ignoring BERT) Start with June 30th, Father. The Regiment left Louvencourt at nine that night. Each man had a 7-inch triangle pinned to his back. It was cut from a biscuit tin and painted red. So the Observer planes could track the 29th in No Man's Land.

ESAU:

Who told you all that? Bert or Sergeant Kelly?

BERT:

Sergeant Kelly.

JACOB:

He said it was 2 a.m. on July 1st when you arrived at the Front. Zero-hour was 7:30 … He said it was hard to sleep with our guns pounding the German lines, the gunners stripped to the waist, some bleeding from the ears.

BERT:

Waiting was the hardest part … There was a page in our pay books for writing a will. I filled it in, then

wrote a letter. 'Dear Folks/Nothing much to report.
Am polishing me boots to go on leave.'

ESAU:

That was a long 5 1/2 hours. I must've smoked a
packet of Woodbines.

BERT:

Someone sang "Tipperary". Remember that? *(To
JACOB)* But not the words Sadie's used to hearing.
(Sings)
'That's the wrong way to tickle Marie,
That's the wrong way to kiss!
Don't you know that over here, lad,
They like it best like this!'

ESAU: *(sings)*
'Hooray pour le Francais!
Farewell, Angleterre!'

BERT & ESAU: *(sing)*
'We didn't know the way to tickle Marie,
But we learned how, over there!'

ESAU:

I minds glancing round at the men, wondering
which would die that day. We called it going West
… It never occurred to me it would be the last I'd
ever set eyes on most.

JACOB:

How could it? No one expected the Regiment to be
wiped out.

ESAU:

… Somehow Will managed to doze off. When he
awoke, he was out of sorts. He'd had a dream he
couldn't shake.

JACOB:

Oh?

BERT:

He never mentioned it to me.

ESAU:

I didn't put much stock in it at the time ... In the
dream he saw a Lee-Enfield jammed in the ground,
bayonet first. On the butt end of the rifle hung his
own helmet and identity disc.

BERT:

The way you and me buried him before the day was
out ...

ESAU:

He said he could read his name and number on it.
As plain as could be.

BERT:

He told you that?

ESAU:

I said, 'Don't be foolish. Sure, lots of men dream
that before a battle. Besides,' I said, 'our Regiment
won't be in the first wave. The Newfoundlanders
and the Essex will be leading the t'ird wave, the
Essex on our right.'

BERT:

I was like you, boy. I figured before it came our
turn the fighting would be over. All but the mop-
ping up ... We all wanted to believe that, I suppose.

ESAU:

The cooks served a hot breakfast at 5 o'clock.
Later, Sergeant Kelly came by with his rum jar and

iron spoon and gave us our ration. Will skipped
breakfast but drank the rum.

BERT:

I remember the sunrise. Seemed like any other to
me. Mist on the blue fields. Not a breath of wind.
Swallows dove over the trenches. Larks sang.

ESAU:

Such a grand day. The sky as blue as the
cornflowers we saw in the fields.

JACOB:

Sergeant Kelly said the Germans had been at
Beaumont Hamel since spring. The
Wurttembergers. A crack division. Tough as nails.

ESAU:

We'd been shelling them all week. 'A rat couldn't
survive that,' Colonel Hadow told us. He was a
British officer, who'd j'ined the Regiment six
months before. 'It'll be a walk-over,' he said.

BERT:

Some walk-over.

ESAU:

The trouble was they'd dug in so deep our guns
hadn't hurt them. Even though all that remained
of the village that morning was some blackened
tree stumps. And bits of walls like broken teeth.

BERT:

The Germans held Hawthorn Ridge, to the left of
the village. The Royal Engineers had dug under the
hill and planted 40,000 pounds of explosives. The
mine went up at 7:20. Ten minutes before Zero-
hour. Made the damndest noise you ever heard.

ESAU:

Almost deafened us.

BERT:

Sent a column of dirt high in the air. Made a crater
60 feet deep ... The worst part was it warned old
Fritz we were coming.

ESAU:

Before the smoke cleared, the Germans rushed out
of the dug-outs and set up their machine-guns, one
on the lip of the crater. They didn't wait long. The
Royal Dublins tried to take the crater but got shot
to pieces ... Then came Zero-hour, and the whistles
went. From our support trench we watched the first
wave of the 29th climb the ladders.

BERT:

The Inniskillings, the Lancashires, the Royals. None
made it far.

ESAU:

The South Wales Borderers got wiped out in five
minutes flat.

BERT:

A damn sin, that.

ESAU:

We saw each regiment start towards the German
lines. Just the way they'd been told to, the red triangle on their backs. We saw them start down the
slight incline of the grassy field, walking in straight
lines, rifles slanted across their chests, the morning
sun glinting off the bayonets. We could hear the
German machine-guns—*tac-tac-tac*—, and the men
dropping in the grass. The guns kept raking the
lines back and forth, back and forth, till scarcely a
soldier was left standing, and those that was looked

stunned … They say it was like that all 18 miles of the Front.

JACOB:
Lambs to slaughter.

ESAU:
At 8:05, the second wave went over the top: the King's Own Scottish and the Border Regiment. They was in the trench ahead of us … Never made it past our wire.

BERT:
My heart was in my mouth the whole time, knowing our turn was next.

ESAU:
It was suicide to attack in daylight. The Germans could see us coming.

JACOB:
Why didn't the Generals call it off?

ESAU:
For a moment, it looked like they had. Our Regiment was set to go at 8:40, but ten minutes before, orders came down to wait. We figured someone in command had come to his senses.

BERT:
In one way the first wave had it easier. At least they believed they had a chance. When it came our turn, we knew the end was near. Even the Colonel looked pale.

ESAU:
At 8:45, the order came down: Newfoundlanders, get ready to advance … Will reached inside his

tunic and brought out Ruby's picture. He pressed his lips to the snap, then tore it up …

BERT:

I don't recall what I did or thought. Perhaps nothing … What does a man do at such a moment? Knowing he's about to die?

JACOB:

What about you, Father? What did you do?

ESAU:

My mind was on Will. It was my fault he was there. My fault he might lose his life. I even considered shooting him in the foot. He wouldn't hear tell of it.

BERT:

No mistake.

ESAU:

He said, 'They'll shoot *you* for that, you crazy bugger. Besides, there's no way I ain't going with the rest of you. No bloody way!'

BERT:

A soldier doesn't die for King and Country, Jacob. He doesn't want to let his friends down. That's why he dies.

ESAU:

At 9:15, the whistles sounded. If you refused to climb the ladder, they shot you on the spot. An M.P. was standing there, his pistol drawn. He walked up and shot you.

JACOB:

Go forward and die. Or stay back and die. Some choice.

ESAU:

We could hear the machine-guns and rifle fire; the mortars. Will was trembling. I said, 'Remember: keep your head down!' And then I helped him up the ladder ... By the time I got to the top, he was walking away. The man beside him bowed his head, suddenly, and crumpled.

BERT:

We hadn't gone twenty yards when Colonel Hadow jumped inside a shell-hole. Only two officers were not killed or wounded that day, the Colonel being one.

JACOB:

You mean he hid, Bert?

BERT:

Some say he was just following orders. Still, he hasn't mentioned the War to this day.

ESAU:

Would you?

BERT:

We had 300 yards of open ground to cross before we reached our front lines. And four belts of our own wire to get past before we made it into No Man's Land. From there it was another 300 yards or more to the German wire ... The guns made so much noise, it was like walking through a storm of sound. We turned our shoulders into it and pushed.

ESAU:

A bullet zipped past my ear like a bee. The man ahead of me yelled, 'I'm hit!' and fell. I stepped over him and kept on going, my eyes on Will. I saw a bullet spark off the steel of his bayonet ...

Somehow we managed to reach our wire. Both of us still alive.

BERT:

The oddest thing happened. As soon as I went over the top, I stopped being afraid. Men were dropping in ones and twos, but I kept right on, heading straight for the gaps in our wire.

ESAU:

The Germans cut us down as we bunched up. Some men got snagged on the wire.

JACOB:

Sitting ducks.

ESAU:

One man struggled to free himself when a bullet struck his face. Another hit an empty sandbag on his belt. It made a little puff of dust the way a baseball will when it smacks into a catcher's mitt.

BERT:

As tough as it was to reach No Man's Land, the worst was still ahead. We knew we were in for it the moment we looked down the field and saw the German wire was still intact. Our 18-pound field-guns had used shrapnel shells. They'd burst in the air but hadn't cut the wire.

ESAU:

Even worse, the Essex was held up at their forward trenches. Which meant the Newfoundlanders had to go it alone, with no support on our right flank. The Germans had us in a cross-fire.

BERT:

I saw two men pitch forward. Then a Whizz Bang cut an officer in two ... I counted my life in seconds.

ESAU:

Will was still ahead. I could see him stepping round a crater. I lowered my rifle and fired at his legs. I missed both times.

BERT:

But don't you see, Esau? Even in the heat of battle you tried to save his life. You mustn't forget that.

ESAU:

A damn lot of good it done him.

BERT:

You did the best you could, sure.

JACOB:

Go on, Father. Tell it.

ESAU:

Before I could get off another shot, a bullet struck my helmet and knocked me flat. My ears rang like I'd been smacked with a crowbar. I took off my helmet and saw only one hole and wondered why I was still alive.

BERT:

The bullet must've spun around inside your helmet.

JACOB:

A miracle.

ESAU:

But why spare me, Bert? Why me and not Will? Why?

BERT:

No one can answer that. Not even the Pope ... I can still see you sitting there, dazed, bullets kicking up dirt like rain. Not a single one had your name on it.

JACOB:

How long did you sit there?

ESAU:

Not long. I climbed to my feet and carried on. A bullet tore the sleeve of my tunic but didn't draw blood ... And then it happened: I saw Will stumble. I figured he'd been shot. Then I saw him pick up his rifle and push on. Seconds later, another bullet spun him around. His arms flew up and down he went.

BERT:

Someone stuck his rifle in the ground to mark where he fell.

ESAU:

The German wire was getting close. I could see the flashes from the machine-guns ... A bullet clanged off the shovel strapped to my back. Made a terrible racket. A piece of shrapnel caught me in the side. I fell to my knees. A bullet pinged off my helmet. Another hit the upper part of my leg. That's when I fell on my face. 'Stay down,' I told myself. 'Don't move.'

BERT:

In my case, a shell landed close by. It lifted me up and tossed me into a hole. That's all I remember till hours later.

ESAU:

Few made it to the German wire that morning. No one lived long enough to boast ... 750 men went over the top. Only 40 answered roll call.

BERT:

Thirty minutes is all it took. Thirty minutes to wipe us out. July 1st, 1916. The First Battle of the Somme...

ESAU:

The Great Fuck-Up, the soldiers called it. Those that lived, that is. The lucky few like Bert and me ... *(He takes a drink from the whisky bottle, then looks at JACOB)* All right, now. I've kept my end of the bargain: I've told you what you wanted to hear. Let's call it a night ...

BERT:

Good idea.

JACOB:

Not yet, Father. You haven't told me all of it ... We still have time.

ESAU:

All of it?

BERT:

Dammit, Jacob, leave him be. He's told you more than he ever intended.

JACOB:

(to BERT) Somet'ing else happened out there in No Man's Land, didn't it? Besides Uncle Will getting shot?

ESAU:

What the hell you getting at?

JACOB:

Didn't it, Father?

BERT:

(to JACOB) Drop it, I said!

ESAU:

What's Bert been saying to you, exactly?

BERT:

I didn't say a goddamn thing.

JACOB:

The sun never set till 9:02 that night. I checked
with Sergeant Kelly … It was a blazing hot day. You
had to lie in that field, along with all the dead and
wounded, waiting for dark … What was that like?

BERT:

What the hell you think it was like?

ESAU:

All day long, I kept seeing Will take that bullet in
the chest. As he spun around, I could see the blood
on his tunic. I saw it over and over … As for me, I
didn't believe I'd last till sunset. A lot of men didn't
… I minds lying in a patch of cornflowers, the sun
burning my neck. I'd fallen next to a dud, an
unexploded mortar shell.

BERT:

The kind we called a 'plum pudding' or 'toffee-
apple'.

ESAU:

Looked like an orange the size of a soccer ball.
Beside it was a poppy. The way my neck was twisted,
I could see the bright red poppy and the big
orange-yellow of the mortar shell. I was t'inking
how beautiful they both looked, each in its own
way, when I passed out.

JACOB:

You probably lost a lot of blood … How long were
you out?

ESAU:

Hours. Minutes. I couldn't tell.

BERT:

When I came to, it was almost noon ... Now and
then an Observer plane flew low. I saw the red,
white, and blue circles on its wings.

ESAU:

Snipers kept picking off anyone who moved. So all
day long I played dead ... The lad from the *Florizel*
was lying close by. One of his ears was shot to
pieces.

JACOB:

Gus Pritchard from Burnt Cove.

ESAU:

I saw him start to scratch his nose. Next I heard the
crack of a rifle ... That's all it took. When he
moved, the sun glinted off the red triangle on his
back and cost him his life.

BERT:

Some men had terrible wounds. One kept saying,
'Shoot me! Someone shoot me!'

ESAU:

The heat was the worst part. I was baking in that
khaki uniform, with those woollen socks and heavy
boots. My t'roat was parched, but I couldn't reach
my water-bottle for fear of being shot. As the day
wore on, my tongue began to swell. It felt like I was
choking ... And just when I figured t'ings could
only improve, that's when the rat showed up.

JACOB:

The rat?

ESAU:

A Somme rat. A big old brown bugger. Well-fed.

BERT:

We had a saying at the Front: The deeper the dug-
out, the bigger the rat ...

ESAU:

The sweat was in my eyes. I'd just blinked, and
there he was, inches away. He was staring into my
eyes, his nose twitching. The brown ones liked
human flesh, especially the eyes and liver.

JACOB:

What did you do?

ESAU:

What could I do? I stared right back. He was trying
to decide if I was dead or not. 'Piss off!' I told him.

JACOB:

Did he?

ESAU:

No bloody way. I figured if I swiped at him, a sniper
would put a bullet in me ... After a spell, he sniffed
at my neck. I could feel his whiskers. Then he
climbed on my back and walked around, heavy as a
cat. At last he began to tear away at my haversack.

BERT:

He wanted the Army biscuits.

ESAU:

All of a sudden he exploded in a red mist. A
German sniper had used him for target practice.

BERT:

Perhaps Fritz didn't care for rats any more than we
did.

JACOB:
> Lucky the sniper was a crack shot. The red mist
> could've been you.

ESAU:
> ... Lying there, I wondered how much longer I
> had. I kept passing out, and each time I did, I
> wondered if this was death, this slipping quietly
> away ... Once I had a dream of home. I saw our
> house from a distance. It was daytime, yet the
> blinds looked drawn. As though someone had died
> ... Another time I was floating above the battle-
> field. I could see the trenches below. They looked
> like white stitches. Like the earth had been
> wounded and stitched up by a drunken cobbler. I
> could make out the dead and wounded. One
> soldier was lying beside an orange shell. He looked
> just like me.

JACOB:
> You?

ESAU:
> Then an R.F.C. plane floated past me, the pilot in
> the open cockpit, his leather goggles on. Barely old
> enough to shave.

BERT:
> Some dream you had, boy.

ESAU:
> It felt so real, too. Not like a dream at all ... And
> then I was in darkness, suddenly, only this time ...
> this time I heard a voice.

JACOB:
> A voice?

ESAU:

It seemed to be calling out to me. Calling my name. Calling me back from that terrible darkness.

JACOB:

Whose voice was it? Can you remember?

ESAU:

I remembers ... It was your voice, Jacob.

JACOB:

Mine?

ESAU:

I hadn't laid eyes on you since that day in St. John's. The day you and your mother came to wave us off. But I swear your face came shining through the darkness, just for a moment, and you said, 'No, Father! No!' ... And suddenly I snapped awake, and the shadow of the mortar shell lay across my face. And the shadow felt cool, like a soothing hand, and I realized I didn't want to die. Not there. Not on that scarred and broken field, so far from home. Not without a fight ...

JACOB:

Why didn't you tell me this before? It might've made a difference.

ESAU:

I'd almost forgotten it. Besides, Jacob, we couldn't talk to each other.

BERT:

Sometimes it's like it all happened to someone else. Sometimes it's like you dreamt it ...

JACOB:
> Go on, Father … It was hours more till dark. How
> did you manage to stay alive?

ESAU:
> I sang.

JACOB:
> Sang?

ESAU:
> Not out loud. In my head. Any song I could
> remember the words to. The filthier the better.
> *(Sings)*
>> 'Do your balls hang low?
>> Do they dangle to and fro?
>> Can you tie them in a knot?
>> Can you tie them in a bow?'

ESAU & BERT: *(sing)*
>> 'Do they itch when it's hot?
>> Do you rest them in a pot?
>> Do you get them in a tangle?
>> Do you catch them in a mangle?'

ESAU & BERT & JACOB: *(sing)*
>> 'Do they swing in stormy weather?
>> Do they tickle with a feather?
>> Do they rattle when you walk?
>> Do they jingle when you talk?
>> Can you sling them on your shoulder?
>> Like a lousy British soldier?
>> DO YOUR BALLS HANG LOW?'

ESAU:
> I also recalled Will in happier times. Like the day
> 'A' Company rested in that orchard outside
> Louvencourt. *(To BERT)* Remember? We all sat in
> the shade and ate apples, even the officers.

BERT:

I've never tasted a better apple since.

ESAU:

A stream criss-crossed the orchard. Made a lovely
sound, bubbling over some stones. Will pitched
apples into a deep pool. Him and some others
stripped off and bobbed for apples. Like kids.

BERT:

Which is what they were, of course.

ESAU:

Just kids ... I figured if I could hang on till dark, I'd
crawl back to our lines. At last I watched the sun go
down, the light so red it was like No Man's Land
was bleeding.

BERT:

As far as the weather went, July 1st was the best day
we'd had so far in France.

ESAU:

Come dark, I slipped off my haversack and took a
drink. Then I tended my wounds with iodine and
field-dressing. I'd just swallowed a morphia tablet to
ease the pain, when I saw ... *(He halts)*

JACOB:

What?

BERT:

Don't be telling him that, Esau. There's no need to
speak about the soldier.

JACOB:

The soldier?

BERT:

No need at all.

ESAU:

Ain't there?

BERT:

No. You've told him more than enough.

ESAU:

Not enough to satisfy him.

JACOB:

What soldier, Father? The one you killed? The one
you took the Luger from? That one?

BERT:

Esau …

JACOB:

Stay out of it, Bert. Let him tell it.

ESAU:

There was a new moon that night, and I could just
make him out. He was walking bent over, stepping
carefully among our dead, making little sounds
with his mouth. It took me a minute to realize he
was calling his cat.

JACOB:

Was he armed?

ESAU:

He had a rifle. It was hard to tell more than that.

BERT:

For the last time, Esau, you don't have to say a
word. No one can twist your arm.

ESAU:

He ain't twisting my arm.

JACOB:

> Go on, Father. You said the German soldier was walking towards you, looking for his lost cat …

ESAU:

> I raised my rifle and took aim. I snapped back the bolt. But before I could get off a shot, he dropped inside a crater.

JACOB:

> He must've heard the bolt.

BERT:

> *(to ESAU)* Don't say I didn't warn you. You're making a big mistake. Mark my words.

ESAU:

> *(ignoring BERT)* I crawled behind young Pritchard, with just my rifle. I propped it on his haversack. I figured Fritz would show himself. It was him or me now, and I'd be damned if I was going to die in No Man's Land. Not after all that had happened … A Very light went up and lit the field around us. I hunkered down. Suddenly a German stick grenade bounced beside me. A metal canister with a wooden handle—good for pitching. I snatched it up and hurled it back at his crater. It exploded in the air … As the flare faded, I crawled behind another dead soldier. I slipped the bayonet off my rifle and rubbed dirt on the blade. I didn't want the steel reflecting light. I smeared dirt on my face and hands. I waited.

BERT:

> Look, what happened that night could've happened to anyone. It was the War … Why not go home now? What's to be gained by telling him this? You'll only be hurting yourself.

ESAU:

He wants the truth, Bert. The whole truth, and
nothing but. Maybe it's time he learned it ... He
can take it.

BERT:

Truth's like a genie, you know. Once it's out of the
bottle ...

JACOB:

He can't keep it to himself forever. It's been six
years since the War ended ... Anyway, I t'ink I know
what happened next.

BERT:

Do you, now?

JACOB:

But what made you do that, Father? Use the
bayonet like a knife?

ESAU:

I don't know why. I'd never killed a man in hand-
to-hand combat. Not even at Gallipoli ... Maybe I
was afraid he'd hear the bolt again. Or maybe I
wanted to make it personal.

JACOB:

You just wanted revenge. The Regiment had been
shot to pieces. You'd seen your brother killed.
You'd been wounded twice.

BERT:

You'd lost a lot of blood. You were probably
delirious.

JACOB:

Frightened to death.

ESAU:

Maybe. Or maybe I went berserk. It happened to a lot of men.

JACOB:

Who could blame you? Look what you'd been t'rough that day ... Then all of a sudden this German appears and tries to kill you.

ESAU:

I was patient. I waited for him to show himself. And whilst I waited, I heard a noise that made the hair on my neck stand up. Soon it was like the roar of a crowd.

JACOB:

What was it?

ESAU:

The sound rose out of No Man's Land like a wail. Like a lamentation ... I sometimes hear it still in dreams.

BERT:

They say you could hear it all along the British Front. Thousands of wounded men. Moaning. Singing out for help. Some crying for their mothers.

ESAU:

And then I heard another sound—a sound that made my blood run cold: the soft scuff of an Army boot. It was nearby, off to my right. I figured Fritz had circled round me, the sly bugger. Well, I could be just as cunning, just as sly. I went, '*Meow!*' but he didn't bite. Then I whispered the only German word I knowed. I said, 'Kamerad?' and waited. It didn't fool him ... didn't draw him out. Instead, he fired. I saw the white flash from the rifle, the bullet whistling past me. I crawled away fast and crept up behind him.

BERT:

Don't do this to yourself, Esau. Jacob already knows you killed the soldier. Let's leave it at that.

JACOB:

Let's not, Bert. He wants to tell it all. Can't you see that?

ESAU:

A cloud slipped in front of the moon. I could barely make him out. He was crouched down, his rifle shoulder-high ... Somehow he must've sensed me, 'cause all of a sudden, he turned and fired. The bullet went wild. I rushed him. Before he could get off a second shot, I rammed the blade in his heart.

JACOB:

Jesus.

ESAU:

I felt the steel go in. He let out a moan. I stabbed him twice more in the chest. The second time I pushed hard and twisted ...

BERT:

Enough ... In the name of Christ, why torture yourself? It's not right ... No son his age needs to be hearing this.

JACOB:

Well, maybe he needs to tell it, Bert. Did that ever occur to you?

BERT:

Don't be a damn fool. It's not for himself he wants to tell it, it's for you ... It's his way of keeping his promise.

ESAU:

I held him tight in my arms. I was afraid to let go. Afraid he had his own knife. I held him there till his legs gave out. Then I sat him down, still holding on ... Another flare lit up the sky, and now I could see his face. His features looked so pale in the light. So young ... *(He looks stricken)*

BERT:

Dear God.

ESAU:

A red foam bubbled from his mouth ... He was looking at me, puzzled. He couldn't speak, but I could see the question in his eyes: *Why? Why had I done this? Why had I killed my own brother?*

JACOB:

What? ...

ESAU:

(his voice breaking) Seconds later, he died there in my arms. July 1st, 1916. *(He turns away)*

JACOB:

Wait a minute ... What did he mean, Bert? His own brother? *(Then)* Bert?

BERT:

(beat) It wasn't the German soldier your father had stabbed, it was Will ...

JACOB:

Will? ...

BERT:

The soldier was already dead. A piece of shrapnel
from the stick grenade had killed him ... Will had
only been wounded that morning. He must've
waited till dark, then set out to look for your father.

JACOB:

He mistook him for the enemy?

BERT:

They mistook each other ... Mistakes like that were
easy to make at night.

JACOB:

Jesus, Bert. And all along I believed ...

BERT:

I know. You thought your father had done
something wicked.

JACOB:

I figured he'd butchered the German soldier.

BERT:

What gave you that idea? The Luger he brought
back from France?

JACOB:

It made sense. I figured he'd done somet'ing there
that he couldn't live with.

BERT:

He had, Jacob. Just not what you imagined.

JACOB:

No.

BERT:

... He was rocking Will in his arms when I stumbled on him. He told me what he'd done. I swore I'd never tell a soul, not even Sadie.

JACOB:

He couldn't look at you after that, could he? Not without being reminded.

BERT:

The sight of me brought it all back.

ESAU:

... I can recall shouting that night: *'Why? Why?'* As if that cold and empty sky gave a damn what we humans did to each other.

BERT:

He'd lost a lot of blood. I had to get him back to our lines ... As it was, our sentries almost shot us.

ESAU:

Bert's too modest. He was lugging me, bent-over, when a German machine-gun opened fire. The bugger didn't even drop me.

BERT:

You would've done the same for me, sure.

ESAU:

Sergeant Kelly said he ought to've got the Military Medal instead of Mentioned in Despatches.

> *Silence. And in the silence the sound of the train whistle is heard, closer now ... JACOB removes the train ticket from his pocket and crosses to BERT.*

JACOB:

Looks like I won't be needing this ticket. Looks like I'm sleeping in my own bed.

ESAU:

You sure?

JACOB:

A deal's a deal ... Father?

ESAU:

What?

JACOB:

Bert was right, you know. What happened that
night was not your fault. After all, you didn't know
it was Uncle Will.

BERT:

Besides, he was trying to kill you.

ESAU:

I've told myself that time and again, Bert. It don't
seem to help ...

JACOB:

Remember what you said tonight? T'ings happen in
war that can never be forgiven ... t'ings a man just
has to live with. It's his punishment.

ESAU:

The cross he has to bear, yes.

JACOB:

Well, I don't believe that. *I* forgive you. Uncle Will
would too, wouldn't he, Bert?

BERT:

No mistake.

ESAU:

(beat) I still can't look Ruby Parsons in the eye. I
don't suppose I'll ever be able to ...

JACOB:

That's why you stopped going to church, ain't it?
'Cause she was there every Sunday, her prayer book
in her lap. His black-haired Ruby from Bareneed.

ESAU regards JACOB a moment.

ESAU:

Look at him, Bert. The spitting image of Will.
Young Will in the prime of life.

BERT:

The same fire in his soul, too.

ESAU:

When we first came back from overseas, he was just
a boy. *(To JACOB)* You've become a man right before
my eyes. And I never noticed it till now …

JACOB:

I never felt it till now, Father …

*The train whistle is heard, even closer … BERT takes
out his pocket watch and checks the time.*

BERT:

Ever hear this one, Jacob? … A Conductor on the
Caribou spies a woman in labour. He says, 'For the
love of God, lady, why'd you board the train, and
you about to give birth?' 'Give birth?' the woman
says. 'Sure, when I boarded the train I was still a
virgin!'

All three men laugh.

BERT:

You know, Esau, last summer Sadie and I took a trip
to England. She wanted to visit her family. While we
were there, I went alone to France. To the Somme.

ESAU:
>   Oh?

BERT:
>   It was July, and the field that sloped down to the
>   German wire was green with grass. There were
>   daisies and buttercups, poppies and cornflowers.
>   Beaumont Hamel had been rebuilt. And in the
>   valley wheat and corn were growing. In the trees
>   there were black birds.

ESAU:
>   Rooks.

BERT:
>   Each spring, the farmers plough up shells and bits
>   of bone. But all that will end one day. And then
>   there'll be just the fields again, and the blue hills,
>   and the bright flowers of summer ... After all, Esau,
>   the Somme is just a river. An ordinary little river ...
>   You know that, don't you?

JACOB:
>   *(beat)* Father?

ESAU:
>   I still minds the march to the Front that night, with
>   the white dust rising on the road, and the men
>   singing. *(To BERT)* Remember? *(Sings)*
>>   'Overseas there came a pleading,
>>   "Help a nation in distress!"
>>   And we gave our glorious laddies,
>>   Honour bade us do no less.'

ESAU & BERT: *(sing)*
>>   'For no gallant Son of Britain
>>   To a tyrant's yoke shall bend,
>>   And a noble heart must answer
>>   To the sacred call of Friend.'

ESAU:
>I can still see the light, you know. The last light of
June bleeding from the sky, Will ahead of me,
trudging on, his head bent. The Regiment
marched across the fields, the men strung out in a
single line, still singing. And the closer we got to
the Front, the louder the guns sounded, and the
louder we had to sing. *(Sings louder)*
>>'Keep the home fires burning,
>>While your hearts are yearning.'

ESAU & BERT: *(sing)*
>'Though your lads are far away
>They dream of home.'

ESAU & BERT & JACOB: *(sing)*
>'There's a silver lining
>Through the dark clouds shining.
>Turn the dark cloud inside out—
>Till the boys come home!'

Blackout.